Hello, Forever Home? It's me, Kona

Peggy Ducky

Printed in USA

A special thank you to Brooke Vitale for her amazing editorial work.

ISBN: 978-1-09836-166-2
ISBN eBook: 978-1-09836-167-9

For my sweet boy, Pee Wee, who is happily playing and patiently waiting at the Rainbow Bridge

Aloha!

My name is Kona.

For a long time, I lived at an animal shelter. I did not like it there.

Even though the people were nice, it just didn't feel like home.
The shelter was too noisy. There was never enough room to
run around. Being in a cage was so sad and lonely.

Sometimes I stayed up all night, wondering when
I would find my forever home.

KONA's BED

Treats

Dental chews

But now everything is different! I have a new mommy!

Isn't that amazing? My life is the best!
I hope I can stay with her forever.

My mommy likes to paint.

Aren't these colors beautiful?

Red, orange, yellow, green, blue, indigo, and violet.

Oh, no!

What a mess. The colors are all over my face. And these paints don't erase!

Uh-oh. What if Mommy is mad. Will she send me back to the shelter? Is this not my forever home?

Mommy just laughs. "It's okay, Kona. I love you in your own way.

Now, how about a bubble bath?"

There's Mommy doing yoga.
How does she hold those poses?

Namaste

KEEP
CALM+
YOGA
ON

Tree pose, triangle pose, warrior
pose, and cow pose. Oh, look.
She's ready to play with me! Here
I come, Mommy. I can't wait to
jump on her and lick her face.

My mommy is the best baker! Don't these desserts look delicious?

Sugar cookies, vanilla cupcakes, blueberry muffins, and a strawberry pie. They smell amazing! I'm sure she won't mind if I take just one little bite since she is busy cleaning.

Mommy just pats my head. "It's okay, Kona. I love you in your own way. Now, here's your favorite chew toy so you're not bored."

Uh-oh! Mommy does not seem happy
about having a spider in the house.

Will she send me back to the shelter?
Is this not my forever home?

Mommy just calmly says,
"It's okay, Kona. I love
you in your own way. Now,
let's trade. A dog biscuit
for the dead spider."

My mommy loves gardening. Aren't these flowers amazing?

Look at these roses, lilies, sunflowers, and daisies. The best part of the garden is the dirt. I love digging and making nice big holes.

Oh, no!

I crushed some flowers while I was digging. Uh-oh! Will Mommy be mad that I ruined her flowers? Will she send me back to the shelter? Is this not my forever home?

KONA'S PIT

Mommy just picks me up. "It's okay, Kona. I love you in your own way. Now, how about a fun digging sandpit just for you?"

As I snuggle into my soft bed, my mommy comes over to say good night.

Oh, no!

Why is she taking off my collar?

Did I do something wrong? Uh-oh! Am I going back to the shelter? Is this not my forever home?

But Mommy just kisses me. "It's okay, Kona. I love you always, and you are here to stay." Then she puts a new collar on me. It has a tag hanging from it:

KONA

IF LOST, PLEASE RETURN HER TO
520 PLUMERIA STREET. SHE IS
MY FOREVER GIRL.

The End

But wait! Kona has something else to say...

A friendly note from Kona:

Prevent your pet from ending up at the animal shelter:

- Be sure your pet wears a collar with a tag stating his/her name and your contact info.

- Microchip your pet.

- Always keep your pet on a leash when outdoors.

- Don't leave your doors open at home, and make sure the gates are secured in the yard.

- Understand owning a pet means keeping the promise to love and take care of your pet for the rest of his/her life.

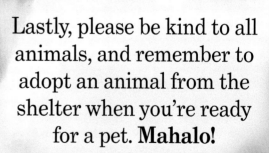

Lastly, please be kind to all animals, and remember to adopt an animal from the shelter when you're ready for a pet. **Mahalo!**